JEN-AI CHILDRESS

THIRTY DAYS
of Loving You

WHEN LIFE ISN'T FULL OF ROSES AND GLITTER

Copyright © 2019 by Jen-Ai Childress

All rights reserved. No part of this publication may be reproduced, distributed or transmitted in any form or by any means, without prior written permission. This work is solely for personal growth. It should not be treated as a substitute for professional assistance. In the event that you are in any physical or mental distress, please contact the appropriate health professionals.

Jen-Ai Childress/www.lovejenai.com /The TariqSphere Publishing.

Washington, DC/20019

Cover Design/Interior Design by:
Yvette E. Tariq | www.thetariqsphere.com | TariqSphere Publishing Concierge

Thirty Days of Loving You: When Life isn't Full of Roses and Glitter -- 1st ed.

ISBN 978-1-7923-1431-5

Thirty Days of Loving You is a sophisticated interactive journal to help peel away the pain and begin to understand the steps of loving you. As each page unfolds you will examine the inner you. This journal is a great way to detox your mind, body and soul. Self-love is one of the most important aspects of your life that will empower you to grow in so many ways. The key to self-love is being able to challenge yourself daily. I encourage you to take the time and dive into Thirty Days of Loving You.

> **Some storms come to disrupt your life, and some come to clear the path!**

Some storms come to disrupt your life, and some come to clear the path! Be patient because the result is more powerful than the actual storm.

What path has been recently cleared in your life for you to walk confidently through without fear or hesitation?

_____
_____
_____
_____
_____
_____
_____
_____
_____
_____
_____
_____
_____
_____
_____
_____
_____

"If you must look back, do so forgivingly, if you must look forward do so prayerfully."

"If you must look back, do so forgivingly, if you must look forward do so prayerfully. However, the wisest thing you can do is be present in the present...gratefully." -Maya Angelou

Name a moment that you are most grateful for, and would not mind reliving a time or two again.

_____
_____
_____
_____
_____
_____
_____
_____
_____
_____
_____
_____
_____
_____
_____

Why are you chained to your past?

Why are you chained to your past? Name a few things that you need to let go of in order to move forward healthily.

_____
_____
_____
_____
_____
_____
_____
_____
_____
_____
_____
_____
_____
_____
_____
_____
_____
_____
_____
_____

It's time to disconnect! Take fifteen minutes for yourself! Sit in silence.

"Silence can never be misquoted."

Silence can never be misquoted. Everyone has experienced being misunderstood no matter how hard the attempt may have been to communicate otherwise. How did you overcome a moment of misunderstanding?

_____
_____
_____
_____
_____
_____
_____
_____
_____
_____
_____
_____
_____
_____
_____
_____
_____
_____
_____

What is your SILENCE? Write five thoughts you experienced in your silence.

_____
_____
_____
_____
_____
_____
_____
_____
_____
_____
_____
_____
_____
_____
_____
_____
_____
_____
_____
_____
_____
_____
_____
_____

"Sometimes when the people you love hurt you...It's better to be silent!"

Sometimes when the people you love hurt you...it's better to be silent! If your love was not enough why would your words matter now. Name a moment when you were proud to just be quiet.

_____
_____
_____
_____
_____
_____
_____
_____
_____
_____
_____
_____
_____
_____
_____
_____
_____
_____
_____
_____

What is your biggest struggle with loving yourself?

List from greatest to least ten things you need to detox from your life:

10.

9.

8.

7.

6.

5.

4.

3.

2.

1.

Detox!

What is the most lovable thing you have done for yourself?

Sometimes the worst place you can be is in your own head. Write down the three thoughts that pop into your mind.

Do these thoughts have a direct impact on your life?

The *Beauty* of it all is how we are calm in the storm and so anxious in the quiet.

I am...

I AM AMAZING!
I AM WORTHY!
I AM SO PRECIOUS!
I AM ENOUGH!
I AM LOVABLE!
I CAN LOVE!
I CAN BE LOVED!

_____
_____
_____
_____
_____
_____
_____
_____
_____
_____
_____
_____
_____
_____
_____
_____
_____
_____
_____
_____
_____
_____
_____
_____
_____
_____
_____
_____
_____

How valuable is your peace of mind?

How valuable is your peace of mind?

Remember there is power in peace, your sanity can be found there.

_____
_____
_____
_____
_____
_____
_____
_____
_____
_____
_____
_____
_____
_____
_____
_____
_____
_____
_____
_____

"If it costs you your peace it's too expensive."

If it costs you your peace it's too expensive.

What do you need to rid yourself of for the sake of your sanity?

_____
_____
_____
_____
_____
_____
_____
_____
_____
_____
_____
_____
_____
_____
_____
_____
_____
_____
_____

What does your *Peace* look like?

_____
_____
_____
_____
_____
_____

What does your *Peace* feel like?

_____
_____
_____
_____
_____
_____

What does your *Peace* sound like?

_____
_____
_____
_____
_____
_____

Questions

INHALE CONFIDENCE EXHALE DOUBT

Inhale confidence. Exhale doubt.
Start each day with a grateful heart.

_____
_____
_____
_____
_____
_____
_____
_____
_____
_____
_____
_____
_____
_____
_____
_____
_____
_____
_____
_____
_____
_____
_____

Learn to be the love you never received! *You deserve it.*

Why would your younger self be proud of you today?

> "The moment you choose not to allow an event, situation, or person to control your emotions is the moment you have accomplished INNER PEACE!"

Discuss an instance that pulled you out of character. Take note of the situation, and identify the emotions you experience right before you feel yourself going down that path. Develop the ability to stop yourself before you start. You've got this.

_____
_____
_____
_____
_____
_____
_____
_____
_____
_____
_____
_____
_____
_____
_____
_____
_____
_____

Healing is an ART!!! Trust the process.

Healing is an ART!!! Trust the process. It takes practice. It takes self-love.

What are you willing to do to see yourself through the process?

_____
_____
_____
_____
_____
_____
_____
_____
_____
_____
_____
_____
_____
_____
_____
_____
_____
_____
_____
_____

flaw•some
[flôsəm] *adjective*

The art of embracing a flaw with confidence, high self-esteem, and no regard for outside approval.

Define your Flawsomeness

You are not here to be average! Step out of your comfort zone and begin to soar. List 10 ways you can begin your fearless journey:

1.

2.

3.

4.

5.

6.

7.

8.

9.

10.

Be Fearless!

You are CAPABLE of AMAZING THINGS. List ten things you are capable of accomplishing with confidence!

1.
2.
3.
4.
5.
6.
7.
8.
9.
10.

Be Accomplished!

Excellence is not being the best, but it is doing your best each and every single day that you are given a chance at life.

"BE STRESS FREE"

Stress is not what happens to us, it's our response, and responses are something we can choose. So, choose wisely!

How will you be stress-free today?

_____
_____
_____
_____
_____
_____
_____
_____
_____
_____
_____
_____
_____
_____
_____
_____
_____
_____
_____

You have the power to change your story!!!
Start Now...

_____
_____
_____
_____
_____
_____
_____
_____
_____
_____
_____
_____
_____
_____
_____
_____
_____
_____
_____
_____
_____
_____
_____
_____

Meditate

You only have two choices in life:

EVOLVE
OR
REPEAT

60 MINUTES OF MEDITATION

FOCUS ON YOUR EVOLUTION

GIVE YOURSELF UNCONDITIONAL LOVE.

Start loving your sarcasm

Start loving your awkwardness

Start loving your weirdness

Start loving your habits

Start loving your uniqueness

Start loving your dreams

Start LOVING YOU

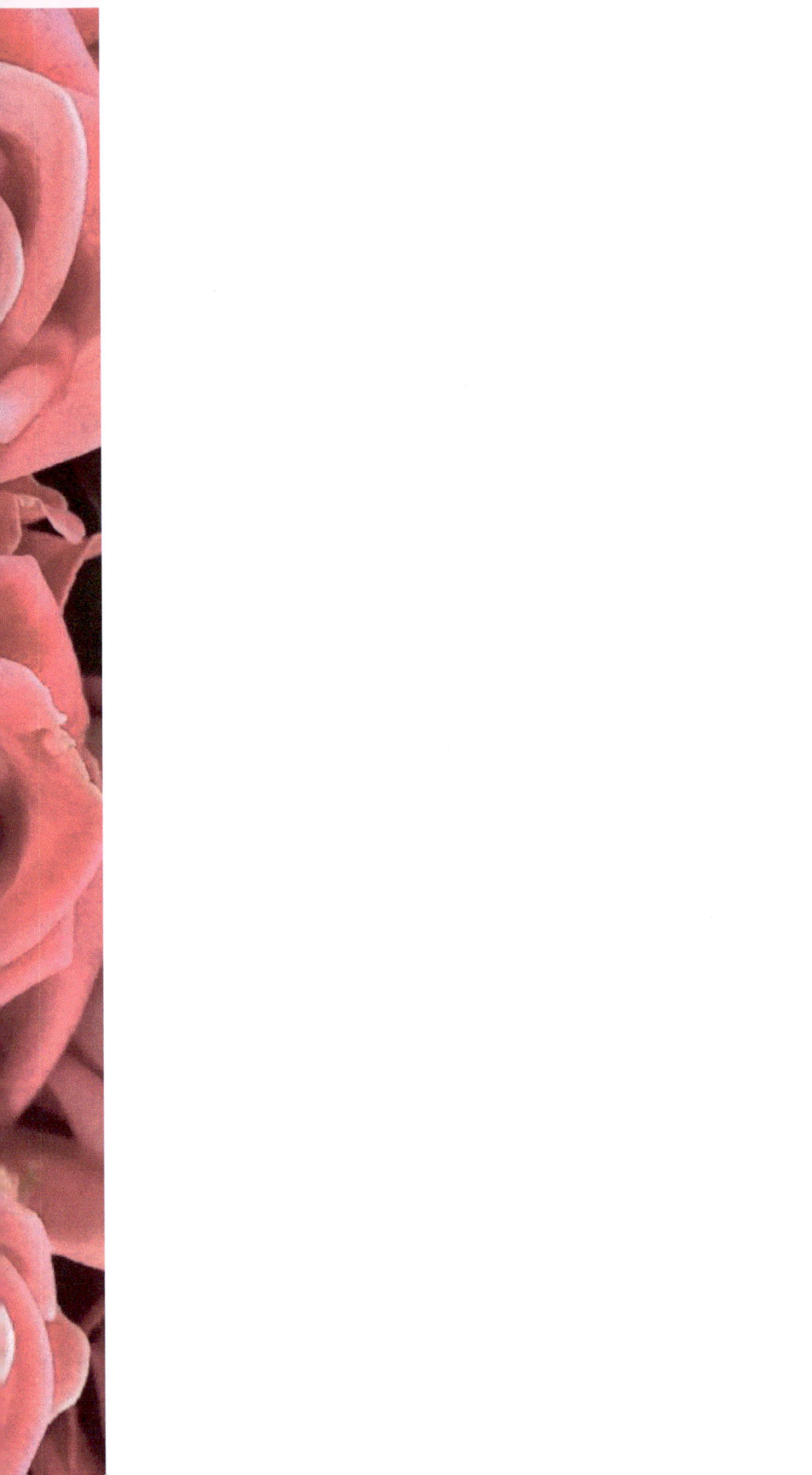

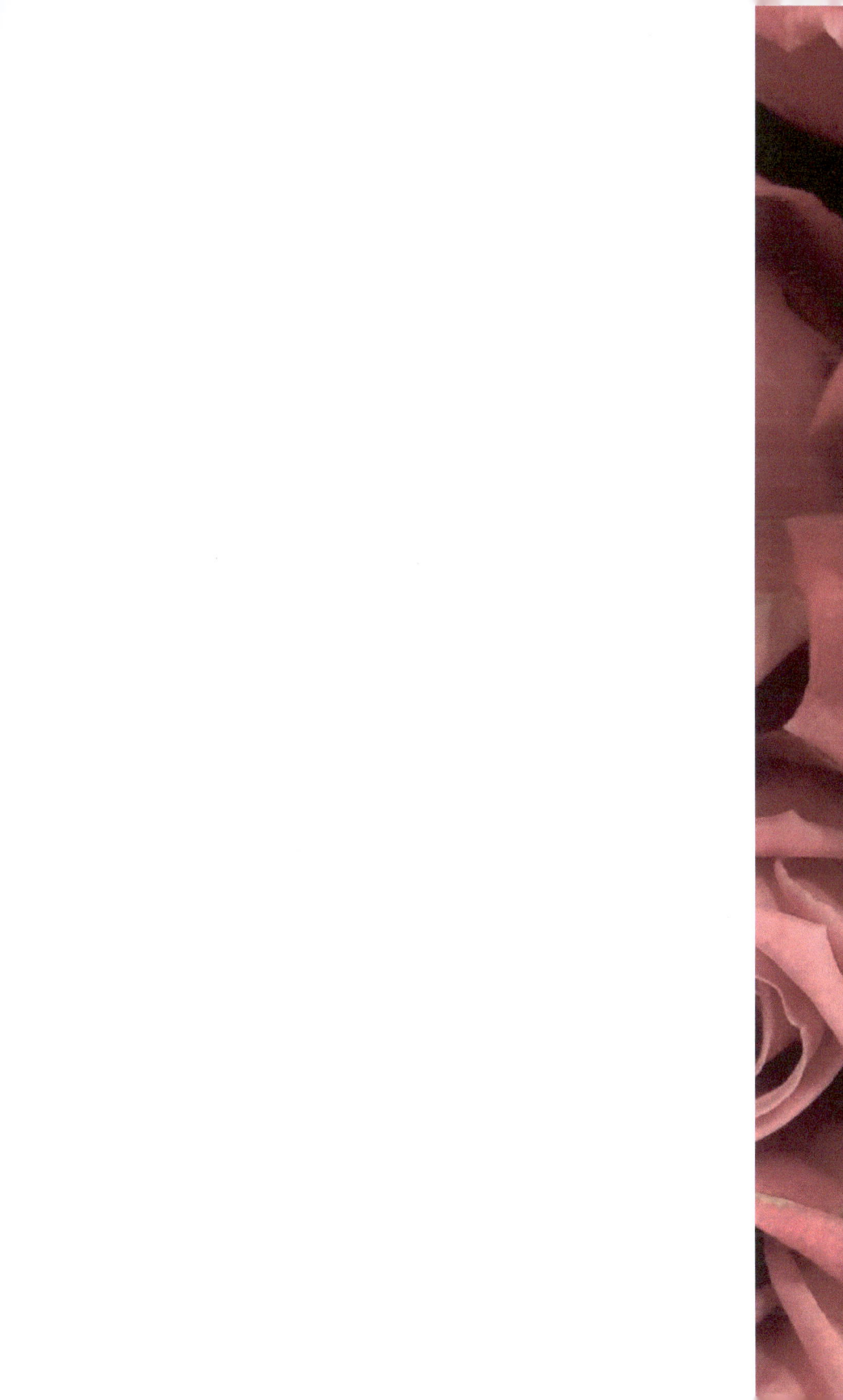

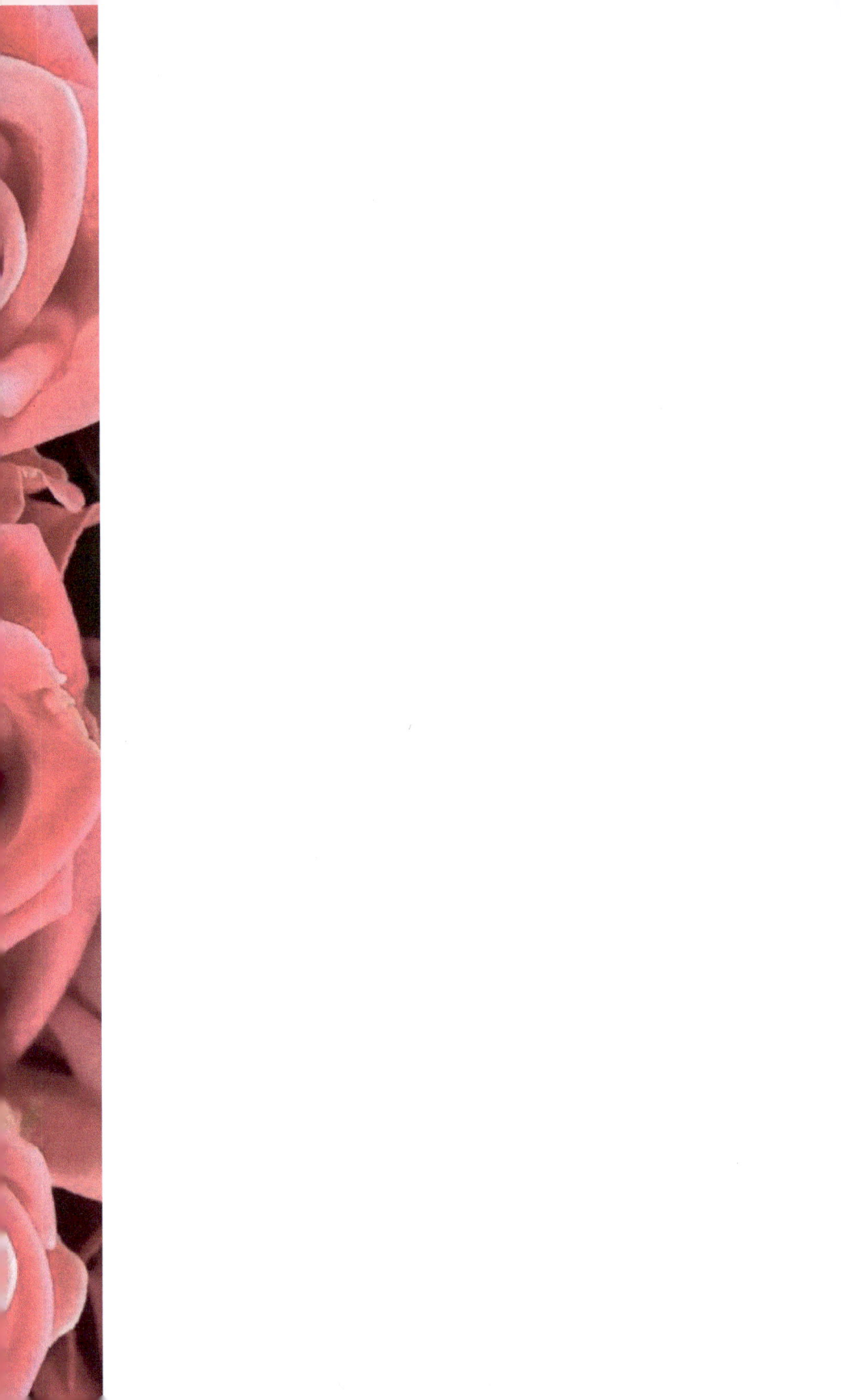

SELF-LOVE
AFFIRMATION

SELF-LOVE
AFFIRMATION

SELF-LOVE
AFFIRMATION

SELF-LOVE
AFFIRMATION

SELF-LOVE
AFFIRMATION

SELF-LOVE
AFFIRMATION

JEN-AI CHILDRESS

JEN-AI IS AN EDUCATOR AND CHILDREN'S AUTHOR. HER PASSION FOR EDUCATION IS EVIDENT IN HER WORK. IT DERIVES FROM HER PROFESSIONAL AND LIFE EXPERIENCE. JEN-AI'S LIFE WAS IMPACTED BY SEVERAL TRAUMATIC EVENTS THAT ALLOWED HER TO BEGIN A JOURNEY OF SELF-LOVE. WHILE OTHERS ANTICIPATED HER FAILURE, SHE USED THAT ENERGY TO REFOCUS AND REBUILD HER LIFE. JEN-AI OFTEN SHARES WITH OTHERS THAT IN ORDER TO BEGIN THE JOURNEY OF SELF-LOVE ONE MUST FIRST EMBRACE AND TRUST THE PROCESS.

WWW.LOVEJENAI.COM